YESSIR, I'VE BEEN HERE A LONG TIME

Also by George Mitchell

BLOW MY BLUES AWAY

I'M SOMEBODY IMPORTANT

YESSIR, I'VE BEEN HERE A LONG TIME

The Faces and Words
of Americans
Who Have Lived a Century

GEORGE MITCHELL

E. P. DUTTON & CO., INC. · NEW YORK · 1975

Published simultaneously in Canada
by Clarke, Irwin & Company Limited, Toronto and Vancouver
ISBN: 0-525-23900-6

Library of Congress Cataloging in Publication Data

Mitchell, George, 1944—
    Yessir, I've been here a long time.

    1. United States—Biography.   2. Centenarians—
United States—Biography.   3. Interviews.   I. Title.
CT215.M57   1975   920'.073   75-16182

3-3-76

DESIGNED BY JEANETTE YOUNG

In Memory of Ampmama (George Smith Stubbs)

I want to thank the following: my wife, Cathy, who assisted me in interviewing and spent many sweltering hours in an unairconditioned bathroom printing the pictures during the summer; the many newspapermen and nursing home employees who led me to the people in this book; Tom and Alison Ceplikas, and Roger and Germaine Brown, who welcomed me into their homes while I was working on this book; and Olive George, who introduced me in one day to the first two centenarians I had ever met, thus giving birth to the idea for this book.

And most importantly, the old people themselves, and their relatives, who so warmly received me and gave so graciously of their time and energy.

George Mitchell
Atlanta, Georgia

PREFACE

No one in this book was born later than 1872. Ulysses S. Grant was President of the United States. The world then was a radically different place from the world now. There were no electric lights, telephones, automobiles, televisions or jet planes. People still lived mostly in rural areas, for farming was the major way of life. People died where they were born, and families stayed together.

The men and women on these pages give a personal account of the history and changing values of this country. They are living testimonies to the way the human mind endures, adapts, changes and transforms. No matter what technological breakthroughs or social revolutions occur, people continue to be people.

I located the centenarians by contacting newspapers, which usually run features on local residents who reach the age of 100. I was led to some by friends, others by nursing homes and, in several instances, by people I had already interviewed and photographed who knew of others in their area.

The photographs were taken with a 35-mm camera without any artificial light, since it might have disturbed the subjects. The interviews were tape recorded, then edited. Everyone in the book was photographed and interviewed in 1972, and their ages are given for that year.

YESSIR, I'VE BEEN HERE A LONG TIME

Mrs. ELIZABETH HULL

WEDOWEE, ALABAMA

My mother died when I was nine months old. My grandmothers on both sides and some aunts taken me and raised me. I came up without the love of a mother, but they were so good it always seemed like they was Mama. Yeah, they was mighty good to me. One of the ones that took care of me, an aunt, she was married and she had a baby that was nursing and he had one breast and me one. A lot of strangers just thought we was twins, but we was just cousins.

The earliest memories I can remember about when I was a child was making snuff. I was just a little kid. They would raise their tobacco, and they'd parch it and fix it and put it in a big old rag, and I'd get out yonder to the flat rock they had in the yard to set your washpan on, and I'd get out there with a hammer and beat it up fine. They would all cough themselves to death when they were beating it, but I wouldn't. After I beat it, they'd fill up their vessels full and give me that real fine stuff in the bottom of the rag, and that's what made me a 'bacco worm. I used to dip, smoke and chew. I had it all. But I had to leave it all off, all but my snuff. I still dip my snuff.

I've had to stop doing a lot of things I used to do, but I'm not going to give up until I just have to give up and stay in the bed. I'm going to go just as long as the Good Lord gives me strength. Let me go! Don't tie me down here and just make me stay in one place! I want to get out and see the flowers and the birds and the bees and be out in the open air.

Some of the happiest times I used to have was when I'd be by my lone self, and I'd get my Bible and my songbook, and I'd be just as happy in my home—nobody but me—as I ever was in a church or anywhere else. But now I can't see to read, and so I can't read to pass off the time. The time seems mighty long, too. My son and daughter-in-law live here with me, and I'll get them to give me something or

13

nuther that I can ravel and tear up and fix and make a mess out of to pass off the time, I get so lonesome. I can get outdoors to walk about a little, but I can't hold out long. Go across the road to the garden and back, then I'm just tired down. Have to get to a chair, sit down and rest. Yeah, Lordy.

Lots of times I sit here and I think back when I was just a child, and I can see the old homestead, the old places, the wells and all the things that was there when I was a kid coming up. I have my imagination now; I can see a lot of them places where I was when I was just a child. Yessir. Down ten miles below Goodwater—that's where I was mostly raised in my child days—and I study about that old place down there now. There was a row of cedar trees in the front yard, a bench under them. I can see them cedar trees and that bench there now. And the well stood around this away, and it was a big oak tree stood there. Now I can't see them, but I imagine I can see them just like I could when I was there.

Yessir, I've been here a long time. I won't be here that much longer now. No, it can't be that long. But I want to stay here just as long as the Good Lord will let me. Whenever he sees fit to call my number, I want to be ready to go. That's just the way I am. Of course, I'm glad to be here where I can see my friends and my children and talk with them and enjoy being with them. But we've all got to go someday, and the thing we've got to do is try to be prepared and ready. For it's a'coming sometime or nuther; it may be in the day, it may be

in the night, we may be on the road; we don't know. But we do
know it's coming to one and all, sometime.

The Lord's got his work for us to do and when we complete
what he aims for us to do, then He's going to call us home. Whenever we complete what He aimed for us to do, then we're going up
yonder—where there won't be no more sad farewells, no more sor-
row, no heartaches and pain—all be peace and love.

My husband's been dead a good long time now. I've got it down
in my Bible, I think it was in '45. But I see him every once in a while.
Last time I seed him, he come back, he was right out there in the
yard. Had on his coat and his hat, and looked like he was trimming
his fingernails or trying to get something out of his finger; I seed him
just as plain. And I went to him, and I was asking him how he was
getting along, and he said, "Very well. How are you?" I said, "'Bout
like common." Then he was gone again. He come back where I can
see an imitation of him. He's coming at me some of these days, and
I'm going to go with him when he comes after me. Folks may say
that's crazy talk, but it ain't; it's a warning or something or nuther to
me that he keeps coming back. And he's gonna come one day and
I'm gonna go with him.

Yessir, Lord, I sure do miss him. Yeah, I miss him. Oh me. We
always will miss them when we lose them—we'll always miss them.
But sometimes look like we can feel their presence near us. They
ain't forgotten us; we all gonna be together again some day or nuther.

15

Mrs. MARY HARPER
NEW YORK, N.Y.

I was the first woman to drive a car in Philadelphia. Back then, women were not driving, you know. Well, the boys on the street used to holler at me, "Get a horse! Get a horse!" I loved it. I wanted to prove that women were valuable in the field of mechanics. The Stanley Steamer—that's the only car I would drive, and you had to know how to repair them because on the road there were no Stanley Steamer repair shops. That was a lone car, not like these other cars, you know, that had shops in different towns. And I would drive all over the country with my husband—my husband was a Quaker, a *Quaker;* don't forget that—and so I had to know how to repair the Stanley Steamer. There was no other way out. That's one reason I got to go everywhere. I knew how to repair. My father was a surgeon—that's where I got my mechanical ability. My father was a surgeon in the Nashville, Tennessee, hospital. He was a surgeon during the Civil War.

The Stanley Steamer, that was a car. It was lighter and took less fuel. There were only three things you had to have: water and oil and fuel. And Stanley furnished the machinery. It was a great car. I have a picture an artist drew for me of Stanley climbing the pyramids. They had what you call traction. That means the contact of the automobile with the earth.

My family was very much pleased with the blessing of cars. An automobile was one of God's blessings. It was a great asset and especially with steam. Steam was an unknown power at the time for cars.

One point. Ford was the liberator of the farm woman. You know, many farm women—not many, but some—lost their minds by not being able to get out. By not being able to get off the farm sometimes. But they became able to on account of Ford making a cheap car. Ford was the liberator of the farm woman. That's another subject.

I want people to believe in God and be a servant of God. And be grateful for their living in such marvelous times.

Do you think these are good times to live in?

It's wonderful to live at any time and enjoy the beauties of life.

What do you attribute your old age to?

The love of people. Love, love of people. Love and interest in life. They all think I took something to make me live so long, you know. I said no, just an interest in life. If everybody would keep interest in their surroundings, if they would only be interested in their neighbors, they would live longer.

I don't want to die. I would love to keep living. I want to live to warn the children of the terror of this opium business. You know, that's an awful thing that's facing the young people. I want to show them the terror of it, and that they belong to God, and that they must continue living in the future to show their gratitude to God. You know, there are so many things yet to be invented. Science! Even the taking of pictures—what a science that is! Science is the *heighth* of intelligence. The heighth. What do you think of going to the moon? Some people think that's not very good. Well, I think if it's God's will, it is good, and He's certainly taken care of the men that have gone up there.

Yes, I'm wearing a wig. I bought me a wig. I went against my friends' protests. They wanted me to stay just like I was. But I said no.

Mr. CHARLIE SMITH
BARTOW, FLORIDA

Charlie Smith lives on Palmetto Street in Bartow, Florida. He remembers being tricked into boarding a slave ship in his native Liberia and brought to the United States to be sold. Charlie Smith was twelve years old when his mother gave him permission to go see the ships docked near his home. Today, he is believed to be the oldest person in the United States. Mr. Smith, who lives alone in a broken-down block house, still talks about how one day he suddenly found himself en route to a foreign land.

There was this man from a different country that had brought his boat to the boat landing where we were, and I asked Mama could I go down to the boat landing, see that man. She said yeah. And I went down to the boat landing, and I ain't never gotten back. All I wanted to do was to see the man. The other people was going down there and carrying the children. And they got on the boat; the man fooled us on the boat. And not just me—everybody.

He was telling us to come onto the boat—"COME RIGHT HERE. COME RIGHT IN HERE AND SEE THIS." They had these little trees on the boat that was kind of decorated just like you decorate a Christmas tree over here now. "OH, WE GOT A COUNTRY WHERE YOU AIN'T GOT TO WORK. WHEN YOU GET HUNGRY, GO TO THE FRITTER TREE." And we all went over to see those little old trees what they had on the boat, had things hanging on them, he pulled one off, said it was a fritter. "HERE THE SYRUP TREE." Here he goes to that tree and pulls something off it, and something like syrup would drop out of it like rain. "THIS IS A SYRUP TREE—YOU DON'T HAVE TO WORK IN THIS COUNTRY—YOU GET HUNGRY, JUST GO OUT TO THE WOODS TO THE SYRUP TREE; IT WON'T COST YOU NOTHING."

19

So then he went down to the lower deck, what they called the hatch hole. "COME DOWN HERE IN THE HATCH HOLE. COME RIGHT DOWN IN HERE." Carried us down there and showed us things down there, and that's when the boat left. When us came back up from the hatch hole, shucks, we was way out in the Atlantic. Not only me—grown people, womens and mens, had the children on there, and they got 'em over here and they sold 'em. They sold 'em.

Mr. Smith was the only member of his family—he lived with his mother and three sisters—to be kidnaped. "I was the only one," he said. "Nobody kin to me, none of my people, were with me. If my mama walked in here now, I wouldn't recognize her." When the young black child arrived in New Orleans to be sold in an auction, he was all alone. With obvious pride, he tells visitors to his home how he escaped actually having to stand on the block.

The man told us, "Put you up on the block, bid you off one at a time." Had a rope stretched all around that block—about as far as clear from here to across the street—and the closer you got to that block the lower that rope was. And everytime they would go to put me up there, Old Man Smith—the man that raised me, the man that gave me my name—he would object. He said, "Don't put that boy up there." I hadn't never seen him in my life till that day and he hadn't never seen me. Well, he said don't put me up there, and by him owning a ranch, having plenty of money, they didn't do it. They ain't bidded on me a'tall. They didn't put me on the block. And when the auction was over, he stepped over that rope and caught me by the hand and carried me to his house, to his ranch in Galveston, Texas.

And he named me Charlie Smith after him—his name was Charles Smith. See, my name, the name Mama named me, was Mitchelwatkins. But Old Man Smith named me Charlie. And I was raised right in his house. I was treated just like one of his children. There was three boys and two girls. There wasn't no difference in the treatment; the only difference in it was they was white and I was black.

Mr. Smith was twenty-one at the time of the Emancipation Proc-lamation, and his owner told him he was a free man. But he stayed on at the ranch as a cowboy until Old Man Smith's death, an event he still describes in detail.

He was dying, and he called for me. And I went in the house, and I said, "What is it?" He said, "Bring me the Bible with all y'all's names in it." I went to the book desk and got the Bible. He said, "Bring me the Holy Bible, I don't want the New Testament." He was sick, laying in the bed. He opened the Bible to Genesis. I was standing up. He said, "Put your hand in here." I put my hand in the Bible. And he read Genesis out, and he turned over to Revelation and read it out. And he was dying, and he said to me, "Don't break your oath, don't change your name, don't change your name," just saying that over and over. But I couldn't understand what he was saying, and I stooped over and he put his arm around my neck. And last thing he was saying, "Don't change your name, don't change your name"— he named me Charlie. And when he quit saying that, he was dead. And I shook him. I said, "Dad?" He was dead.

I went to the door and called his oldest boy and said, "Have the saddles took off the horses and tell 'em we can't go to town." He said, "What's wrong?" I told him the old man was dead. He named me Charlie.

Mr. Smith is not as clear about what he did after leaving the ranch, but he apparently roamed the West as a cowpuncher for a number of years and worked for a while at a logging camp in Mississippi. He speaks of "crossing the sandy desert," of riding with Jesse James, of "being the first colored man ever made a Mason," of "breaking up chain gangs," of being "sent to Miami during the '26 storm to keep the people from robbing all the dead bodies," of "running a still when the comet came," of "straightening up" Florida towns so blacks could live and work in them ("I remember when a colored woman couldn't drive a car in town; Bartow wasn't no churchhouse").

Mr. Smith moved to Bartow at the age of 121. Today he spends most of his time sitting on a brightly painted red and blue bench outside his house, wearing an old military uniform, a bow tie, a lanyard sporting a carved steer head, a John F. Kennedy silver dollar medallion, and a Mason's button. Above the bench is a sign faded to the point that one can hardly read the words: "Charlie Smith, Soft Drinks and Candy Bars." In his front room, posters advertising BC and Goody's Headache Powders adorn the badly chipped walls. On top of a stove in a corner are a few boxes of candy bars and Ex-Lax, the only items Mr. Smith is offering his customers these days. Cases of empty soft drink bottles are stacked along one side of the room, but he stopped selling soft drinks a couple of months ago because, he says, "They went up on the price and I won't pay it."

Mr. Smith seems to enjoy visitors, and he will talk at length about his life.

A whole lot of people reads the history and reads these things and that about the world—that's all they know, what they read—but I don't read mine. I know what was going on.

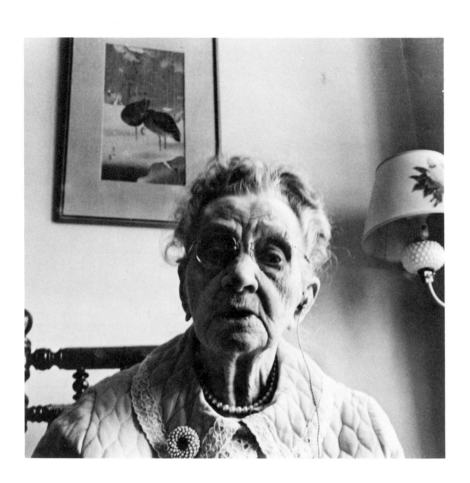

Mrs. SOPHIA DAVIDSON
MINNEAPOLIS, MINNESOTA

The only thing I remember of my childhood is that we lived beside the ocean. And we used to go down and build houses with the pebbles on the beach.

I love my rocking chair. It was a wedding gift, and that was a good many years ago. I have rocked all my seven babies in it, and now I'm rocking myself.

I don't count the years any longer. I just count the days. But looking back, I can count the years.

I always think this may be my last day. And if it is, may it be a good one.

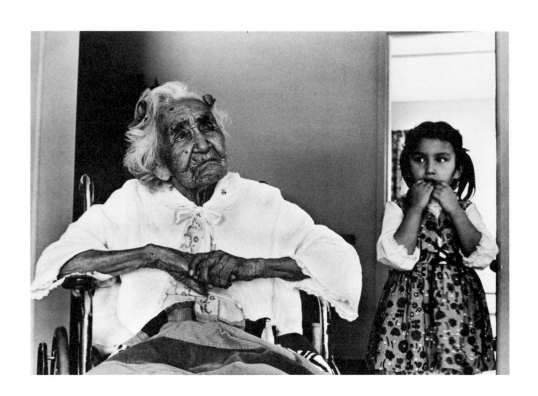

Mrs. NANCY LOSH
GRAND RAPIDS, MINNESOTA

Mrs. Losh's daughter, Mrs. Hattie Hillstrom, tells about her mother bringing up two bear cubs:

When she first got married, she and my dad were living in a wigwam near a river. They had twin baby boys. One day my dad went trapping and found two bear cubs. They were little bitty ones, and he brought them home, and Mother brought them up as if they were her own. She nursed them right along with the twins. They all grew up together, those four. The bears used to sleep with the boys; they all four slept under the same blanket. But when the bears got a little older, they started getting mean. They wrestled under the blankets and made the boys cry. It was a sad day when they took those cubs up the river in a boat and let them out in the woods. And ever since then, Mother has put sugar and candy bars out in the woods.

Mrs. Losh's great-granddaughter, Elaine Sullivan, wrote this tribute to Mrs. Losh, which was read at her 104th birthday party:

Nancy Washington was born at Pigeon River on November 15 in the year 1867.

We are here today to help celebrate her 104th birthday and to recall some of the important events in her long life.

As a girl, she was a great hunter and trapper. When she was in her twenties, she shot a moose.

Later in life, she married William Losh, who was an ordained minister in the Episcopal Church. After their marriage, they both encountered many hardships in their missionary work. They traveled by buggy and sleigh all through the Leech Lake and Squaw Lake area, although their home was in Bena.

At the age of forty-three, she witnessed the passing of Haley's Comet. This comet passes every seventy-seven years and will not be seen again until 1986.

She had sixteen children, and she raised them in the Episcopal faith. She taught them the legends of the Indian people and their own family history.

She took part in the yearly wild rice harvest and maple sap gathering. She tanned deer hides and did beadwork. Her children learned from her many of the Indian ways of living, and she encouraged them to participate in the ancient Indian dances.

She is the eldest of five generations. She has five children, twenty-one grandchildren, seventy-three great-grandchildren and eight great-great grandchildren.

So we congratulate you, Grandma, on your 104th birthday, and God bless you.

When Mrs. Losh cries, they bring her something to beat a rhythm on—maybe a Kleenex box—so she can sing. The tears usually stop then. She sings in Chippewah and makes up the words as she goes. Perhaps she will sing about a "sweetheart in a white shirt":

> You must go home now.
> You get in trouble
> If you stay too long,
> So be on your way.

Mrs. CARRIE FARLEY

EATONTON, GEORGIA

My father was a white man. He owned a big farm. And his mother, Mrs. Tatum, raised me. My mother was a servant. I came right after Freedom, you know, and my mother was a servant, and she lived on the place, and I lived in the big house. My mother was a servant; she waited on them and cooked, washed and toted water from the spring and done everything. She was a servant, a good servant.

I can still remember back then in childhood. White children would come in and we'd play together—go get sweet gum. You know there was no chewing gum in those days. We'd chew sweet gum. Grandmother, that's my father's mother who raised me, she would prune the trees down, let the sweet gum run out, and we'd catch it in a tin box and cook it a little bit, and then we'd chew it. It had a good taste. We'd get sweet gum. It was a big thrill.

Now, people didn't have buggies when I come up. They went in ox carts. Grandmother's daughters what was married off, they'd come see her driving two oxes. A two-wheeled wagon with two cows hitched to it. Well, that's the way people went, even to church. And horseback. I used to be a housegirl for Miss Posey Maddox, and she and her sister used to live about four or five miles from her church. And they had a horse that her brother plowed the farm with. And when they had revival, Miss Posey and her sister would start about one o'clock and walk to church. And their brother would plow till long 'fore night, and then he'd feed his horse, and he'd get on that horse and ride to the church, and them two sisters would ride that horse back home. And he would walk. That's Mr. Mansfield Merritt, and Miss Posey and Miss Dolly was his sisters. And Miss Posey married Mr. Stubbs, Mr. Charlie Stubbs. And Miss Posey's daughter married a Wilson.

Miss Posey was right old when she got married, and when she was single I was a housegirl for her. I was about ten when I started being a housegirl, cleaning up and waiting on tables and all. But when she was single, Mr. Stubbs had gone off to Texas, and when he come back, he come to see Miss Posey, riding on a mule. And she was sitting out on the back steps, and she seen him coming, and she said, "Lord, here comes Charlie." See, she hadn't seen him in a long time—people thought they had done broke up.

Now, she wasn't dressed up, and she wanted to look pretty when she saw Mr. Stubbs. So she told me to go and bring him in and shut the door to the sitting room so she could go upstairs to her room without him seeing her. And she told me when I done brought him in to bring her a pan of water upstairs so she could dress.

So I went and bringed him in, and he asked me, "Where's Miss Posey?" I say, "She's out in the garden." She's really gone upstairs to dress, but they had me trained, you know. So I took his hat and told him to sit down; he sat down. Then I carried Miss Posey a pan of water upstairs, and she dressed. I followed her on down there, and she met him.

Another thing I remember about my childhood days was that we wrote with ink that was made out of oakballs. See, this was when I was going to the colored school that one of Mrs. Tatum's daughters

taught in her kitchen. They didn't have no books for we to read in—
a piece of Bible or anything we could get to learn us something. And
I learned how to write with ink made out of oakballs. We'd get them
balls that come on oak trees and we'd mash them and make ink out of
them. And the old man—Old Man Tatum—would make us a pen out
of goose feathers pulled out of a goose wing. I see those things on
television now—make me think of old times.

Mrs. Tatum's daughter taught school in her kitchen. Had a little
log kitchen out in the yard, and she'd teach colored children three
months out of the year after they laid by the crops. There wasn't no
colored school. And I went three months one year and three months
the next. And that's all the schooling I ever went to.

*How could you work the crops and raise fourteen children at
the same time?*

Old Mrs. Tatum died when I was thirteen, and then I went to live
with my mother. And I got married when I was sixteen. I married
Dan Farley. A farmer, that's what he was. I had fourteen children.
And I never married no more. I and him lived together fifty-four
years. And he's been dead thirty-one.

I couldn't really tell you what the secret is of staying married so

31

long. Just live together and go through hardship. We had some hardships to go through because times was hard. Sometimes we didn't hardly have enough to eat. The only money we got was from the little cotton we could make, and we would have just enough to go through Christmas. Had to do it or die one. But I wasn't always making crops. I started out being a midwife eighty years ago. When I first started out, I just helped the doctor wash the baby, and then later on I started helping birth them. I couldn't tell you how many babies I helped birth. 'Round 300, I reckon, white and colored.

And the first one I ever washed after he was birthed, he died last year at Sparta. I was helping the doctor birth him when he was born, and when he came I washed him. And when he grew up and got married, I worked for his family waiting on them. And he was a big fat boy. And I say, "I washed you when you was a baby." He said, "You'd go blind if you washed me now." And he died last year, and they brought him back to Putnam County and buried him.

Sometimes I was a midwife, and then sometimes I lived in people's houses waiting on them. I waited on a lot of people around here, and I've waited on people in College Park and East Point. And I have white friends up there now that write me sometimes. Now, I worked a week for five dollars and was glad to get it. Cook, wash and wait on that lady. Times was tight, but you know you could buy as much with that five dollars as you can buy with twenty-five now.

Serving the Lord is the most satisfaction I get out of life. I can tell you something to prove it to you. One time I was nursing—you know, waiting on this family—in Florida. And so after I had been working for this family for a while, they didn't need me any more. But there was another lady that lived near them, she wanted me to come and wait on her and her two children. And when we was fixing to leave, the lady I had been waiting on told this lady I was going to work for, "You take care of Mammy, we all love Mammy."

So this white lady that employed me, she was big and fine, and she had a little girl that was two years old. And one day the baby was crying, and I said to this lady, "Miss Rosa, your baby's crying. It's time for nursing." And she was playing with the bigger baby on the bed and she said, "*I* know when to nurse it!" And you know that

hurt me . . . I got my Bible. I said, "Lord, wherever I open, I'm gonna read." And I opened it, and where I read it looked like it was encouragement. See, when the lady said that to me, you know, if I could of flew, I would've come back to Putnam. That's all she said to me. She carried me to help her, and I was trying to help her and she said that, it hurt my feelings. And I read my Bible and I said, "All right."

I never did sass anybody. If they treat me wrong, they didn't know it. What you get out of that? See, when they hurt my feelings, they didn't know it. See, I'd take it to the Lord. Always took it to myself and to the Lord. I never did argue. I have cried a heap of times to myself. I took it to myself. And I'm glad today I did so. See, now I can rejoice in the God of my salvation. And it makes me have friends.

I don't think about the evil things going on 'cause these things must come to pass—the Bible say that. All that's going on—good or bad, but more bad going on than there is good. And, you see, it's got to be. And I just pass it up. I don't worry over it, you know. If they say somebody got killed out yonder, I wouldn't get up and go out there and look at them. It wouldn't do any good. I study good, I don't study evil. And that keeps my mind in good shape.

And I don't ever weep and groan over things I can't help. And when people in my family pass, I say, well, the Lord give, He take away. And I got to go, too. And I pass it up thataway. I don't worry over things. You know when people worry over things, that upset their mind.

I'm going to live just as long as the Lord say, and I may be here when Christ come. He says that some will be here and some will be gone. And I may be here; I don't know.

Miss HELEN HANK
CHARDON, OHIO

I was born in Shaker Heights, Ohio, and there was a stone quarry there. My father worked in that stone quarry—he was the boss—and one day he wanted a stone cut in a different way than this man was cutting it. He wanted to have a certain kind of stone cut to be just such a length—Mother said he always wanted it just so. And so he had it all arranged. And in the quarry there was this man that operated—what did they call it?—the big trolley, I think, what the stone was hung on. And my father wanted that stone cut *just so;* I guess they were going to build something with it. But, anyhow, he told that man to swing that trolley around, and the man wasn't doing it right. So my father takes the big trolley, and he swings it, and that thing on the top broke, and that big stone fell on my father and killed him. That's when my father was killed. And I was two years old.

My mother took such pains in taking care of us, because of our father. He was so proud when he had a family, and she wanted to raise them right, and she took such good care of us, and she raised us. And she went along so many ways that was his wish to be. She always would say, "Oh, if your father was here, how different it would be." But she tried to follow out his footsteps in sending us to school and everything. It was always—"That's what your father would have liked." Too bad that he had to be taken away.

In later years when my two sisters and I were growing up, Mother was very particular in teaching us to sew. So when we got to be about twelve years old, we did learn to sew pretty good. And when we were about fourteen, we learned to make vests, men's vests. Sister Kate was the first one that learned to do the vest making, and she taught me and Anna. And so we started making men's vests, and finally we quit school, and we went and worked in a shop making vests. And we used to take bundles home from this company and make the vests at home and then take them back. I remember taking them down there, carrying them all the way down to the streetcar.

We made vests for this company for many years, and we saved money. And then we built a dry goods store, a small store, and we sewed in it. And later we built a larger store, and then we built another store. And gradually we made money. My two sisters and I were doing this, and Mother did all the cooking and baking and everything for us.

How we used to work at night to get the vests done! Oh, sometimes when we were younger and working for the company, they wanted a certain number of vests done in a certain day, and we had to work nights to get them done. We did a lots to please them. I think that's why they always gave us work.

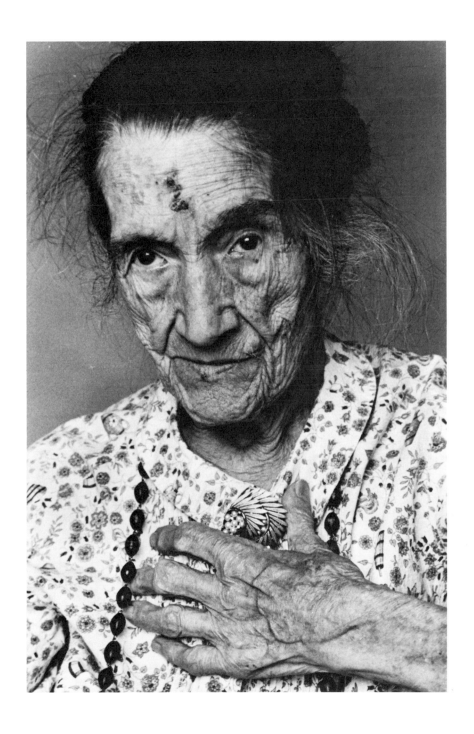

Mr. HENRY LEMON
MASON CITY, IOWA

I was a farmer. Been working in the fields since I came from Indiana to Iowa when I was eight years old. I was a single man, and I always liked farming. Raised corn and oats. Farming in those days was a lot different. You had to go over everything with your hands. Had to cultivate the corn with a hand cultivator. But now they got tractors to do all the work. All you do is sit on 'em.

Mrs. ESTELLE HOWARD
CLEVELAND, TENNESSEE

There was a big rock just sitting there in our front yard. It was when I was a little girl. I never will forget that rock.

I don't know what my father was. I've never seen him. My mother's dead, she never did tell me nothing. My mother died when I was young. I was just turned loose in the world.

I've had a hard time all the way up. Hard work. I've done hard work in my time. I made one crop by myself; I can't give up that good old farming. I was just lone by myself; I always stayed to myself, and then I'd know what I'd do.

God always had my right hand, leading me. I could stand anything that come up. I'd take a hold of anything. Take hold of everything that was good to me and ran.

Yeah, I killed myself doing hard work. I've come out in the kitchen a many a night long ago, shut that door, get my dishes done, then go over and go to bed. That's the way I was raised.

That right hand of mine took every tooth in my head. I ain't got a tooth in my mouth. I got me a pair of wire pliers and just went in and pulled 'em out. I didn't fool with no dentist. I just runned the risk and hoped that God would carry me on through. Yeah, it hurt. Though I can stand it.

I've been here in this nursing home a good bit, but I don't know who runs it or nothing. I don't ask no questions. I just go on and take what they put on me and don't say a thing about it. Keep everything to yourself!

I'm just an old hard-shelled Baptist. Can't make nothing else of me. *Just being able to walk at the age of a hundred is pretty good.* I expect I could run if I had to.

Mrs. CLARILDA ROY
LEWISTON, MAINE

It was very poor in those days when I was growing up in Canada. There was no electricity. It didn't appear very nice, but it was nice. We didn't live in the grand style that people live in today, but we lived just the same, and we grew up like everyone else, and we made our way like people do today. Today cars are speeding and there is television, but it's not much more fun than it was in the past.

I was eighteen when I met my husband. We had always lived close together, but we had never met one another. And he had a brother and I had a sister, and they married both of us—my sister and I. I was eighty-two when I became a widow . . . pretty old.

Are there any rewards of having lived to such an old age?

It's always beautiful, but it's also sad, because I can't find life as beautiful as it was when I was young. My bad eyesight prevents me from seeing a lot of things, and my ears don't hear as well, so I miss a lot around me that I had in my youth.

And my children brought me many joys and also many sorrows. Me, I had twelve children, and they were a great pleasure to raise. But I have lived so old that I have seen nine of them die, and I was very much aware of it.

Yes, if you're looking for old, this is it.

⊰ 102 ⊱

Mr. BOB SHEPHARD

GULFPORT, MISSISSIPPI

Mr. Shephard got married for the second time at the age of 102. He didn't have much to say about his reasons for taking a wife again, so we talked about other subjects.

Can you tell me about your mother?

No, I can't tell you about her, because I done forgot about her. Well, when you're dead, you're just dead. I don't think about you no more. It ain't doing no good thinking about them.

What kind of work did you do?

I was raised up on a farm, and I started farming when I was a little bitty boy. When I got big enough I quit farming and went to railroading. Tamp them ties out there and slag and everything, walk the tracks, and I raised sixteen children.

What has given you the most satisfaction in your life?

Sitting down.

Have you seen many changes during your life?

Stealing and killing. When I was coming up, there wasn't that going on. Uh-uh, no. Folks just don't want to work, and if you give them a job, they don't want it. They'll go and steal something or kill somebody or rob something—they're going to get into some kind of devilment. Running in people's houses, robbing them. One runs in here, and the undertaker man's going to have to come and get him. I don't care who he is—white or black, where he's coming from or where he's going—he come here and open that gate and don't say no more and break in here, I'm gonna kill him. And go and tell the man I done it. I don't bother nobody, and I don't want nobody bothering

45

me. Folks done got terrible now, they done got terrible.

But it don't worry me because I ain't going nowhere nor mess with nobody; I'm gonna stay in this house. I don't go nowhere.

. . . See, when I gets up in age, I don't think about nothing.

Mrs. ELIZABETH McCRARY
ATLANTA, GEORGIA

I came up the hard way. My mother died when we was quite small. She left five children and I was the elder one, and I was just going on eleven years old. And coming up, didn't none of them remember her but me. None of my brothers and sisters would have knowed my mother if she was to come up out of the grave.

Motherless children have a hard pull. After our mother died, our kinfolks just scattered us around different places. We just went from one kinfolk and whoever to another, just shifted us around first to the one and then to another. They ain't like your own mother. We was treated pretty rough. As Grandma say, "You have sucked the hind teat." When all the milk been sucked out, we come up at the hind and get what we can to live on. Yessir.

So we was just children, just come up in the world, by different people. Whosoever would do for us, we'd go to them. Just anybody who would come up and give us a piece of bread and a drink of water. You know, if you was hungry, someone would say, "Give 'em some bread" or "Give 'em some water." I tell children now, "Y'all young people in this day and time got a sugar teat in your mouth, and you don't know it."

Times just changed up. I just sit here and think about it. Folks killing and breaking in people's houses in the daytime and taking things out. I just wonder all about it. I wonder what the people *mean*. I've been here a long time, and I never did hear tell of such carrying on as now, folks just coming into your house in the daytime and taking everything out. I just thinks about all that.

I'm just here. I'm just here in the hands of the Lord. That's all I can tell you. Just here by being obedient, I reckon—I'm just here. I must have done something good, somewhere. He keeps me here. So many have come since I come, and gone. I'm the oldest member of Providence Baptist Church. All of 'em that was baptized in my time is gone—nobody to tell the story but me. I'd be glad to be here a thousand years. So many that have come since I've come have gone and forgot the world.

I'm here, living . . . I ain't no good . . . my mind goes and comes, but I thinks, sometime. My mind goes, but then my mind comes to me, you know. Look like I wonder sometimes . . . just sit down and just get to studying over things . . .

But I must have done some good, somewhere. The Lord keeps me here at this age. Yessir. And you don't know how much I thanks Him. I thanks Him. I thanks Him for being here with breath enough to talk. And if I don't know what I'm talking about, just give me a little leeway. Sometimes my mind goes and comes. I just sit here and think and dream. Just thinking way back, what I have done, wondering. My mind looks like it just goes away and comes back. I think of something, and I get up and think to myself: is that real or did I dream that?

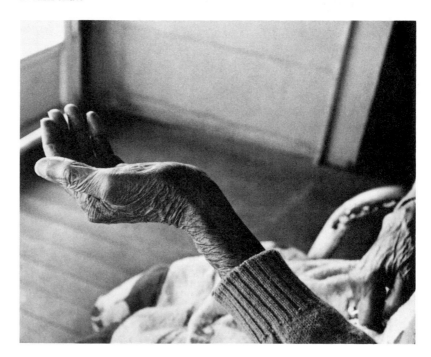

Mrs. JENNIE WHITLOCK KEAN
DERRY, NEW HAMPSHIRE

Whiskey improves with age. I don't improve, but I'm here.

I've been to France, England and Scotland. I've been around. I wanted to be independent. I wasn't going to stay down on the farm and milk cows and make butter.

So I became a furrier. And I had to pick up that trade myself. There was nobody around to teach me. If everything comes easy, you're nobody.

I made the furs from the skins. I made them myself, and I sold them in my own store. I had my own business. It was hard work, too. But I said I was going to have it, and I did.

I was too damned independent to go to work by the whistle. I said I never would go to work by the whistle, and I never did. I said I'd never be whistled in and whistled out. I said if I was worth a day's pay to somebody else, I was worth two to myself.

I've been married three times, and I'm looking for the fourth one. I'm here waiting for him. Well, I won't say I'm looking for a man, but if he ever comes along—oh, boy!—he's done. I tell them I used to have to run so the boys wouldn't pick me up, and now I have to fall down so they will.

If I want to look at a man, I'm gonna look at him. You can't stop me. But of course they don't chase me. But I'm very happy; I've got my own room, and I had my own business.

Mrs. IDA LETCH

ROCHESTER, NEW HAMPSHIRE

I used to speak pieces that I memorized. I would speak them at different places to entertain people. The churches here used to have people come and speak pieces for them. And sometimes when it come bad weather and the one that went regular to some church, he couldn't come, and they'd send after me to fill in. I belonged to their Ladies Aid, you know. They'd send after me. Lots of times they'd say that they were glad that the other one didn't come. And for years we in the Relief Corps used to go up to the Old Soldiers' Home every fall, and I would speak pieces up there. One I used to always tell was about the minister and the sheep. You ain't got time to listen to it, have you?

Well, this is Aunt Melisa's, on boys, what she thinks of boys: I ain't got nothing against boys. They're a necessary part of creation, I suppose, like all other disagreeable things. The Lord deliver me! I'd rather bring up a family of nine gals any day in the week with cats and dogs thrown in, than one boy. Oh, a boy, he's always getting into mischief; he's born in mischief. Climbing trees and fences, tearing his trousers—and it's patch, patch, mend, mend. Now gals never climb trees, tear their trousers.

Now we have no preacher in our town and when we have meeting, they come from out of town. And they ride in on horseback and stay overnight. And so they called them the circuit minister.

Well, this year they chose Old Elder Thomas. Now, Elder Thomas warn't liked by lots of people. It was pretty hard work to get him put up over the weekend. Well, we got a new neighbor who moved into our town by the name of Haynes. And the father is a real live go-to-meeting church member, the mother's one of the best cooks in town, makes the best risen biscuits I ever eat away from home. The gals were pretty gals, well behaved. But that there boy—

53

Larkie. Oh, dear sir, why the mischief was born right in him. It's nothing disagreeable but that boy knows how to do. He'll go down to the creek, and he'll get toads and frogs, snakes, and them big spiders and worms. And he'll come up and throw 'em right down in front of you. And, of course, you jump and holler and scream, scare the life right out of you. Then he'd lay right down on the ground and laugh and roar. His folks never done a thing to quiet him down— they think it's funny.

Well, as I said, we had the meeting. And Haynes, the father in the new family, he liked the minister, Elder Thomas. So he had him stay with him. Well, he generally stayed with him. One time this here boy, he had got a hold of some young lambs, things like that, or hogs. And he'd train 'em to do tricks. And he got hold of a lamb that he trained, and he learned him to run into and butt at things. All he had to do was shake his handkerchief right in front of anything, and that there sheep would run right through and bump anything you had behind it. Wouldn't matter to him if it was at the meeting house. Well, after a while he got to be something more than a lamb—great, tall, long-horned critter. And now I tell you, you wouldn't want to be twice behind that handkerchief and have him run into you and bump at you.

Well, as I say, Elder Thomas generally stopped with the Hayneses. Well, he came this time right in summer. And, you know that's a busy time with the farm folks, right in haying time, and, of course, he stopped at the Hayneses as usual. Well, in the morning the family had eaten their breakfast and drawn back their chairs for family worship, and, of course, Elder Thomas, he was lengthly as usual. And it was terrible hot in that kitchen. But he didn't mind it any, the minister. He had placed his chair over against the cellar door, which was open, and his back to the outside door, which was open, too. And there he knelt right in the draft and praying for all he was worth. And, of course, he was lengthly as usual.

Well, after a while that there Larkie got uneasy. So he looked through his fingers trying to see if there weren't some mischief he could get into. And he looked out the back door and there stood that sheep of his. And that there sheep happened to see Larkie at the same time. Well, enough said. No sooner than he saw Larkie than he picked up his heels and got all ready to come right in. And Larkie

54

took out his handkerchief, shook it careful right behind the Elder's back. Well, in he come, head over heels and straight for that hand-kerchief and the kneeling elder. Well, there was a thump and a bump, and the elder, his chair and that horned critter all went roppity-clock right down the cellar stairs. Such an interruption to family devotion.

Haynes happened to look up just in time to see the elder's boots, the legs of that chair and the hind tail of that horned critter shooting out of sight. He made a rush for the cellar, expecting nothing but to find the elder half dead with his neck broken. But when the elder fell down them cellar steps, he went head-first right into a firkin of soft lard. And when Haynes pulled him up by the boots, his wig stuck fast. And he was as bald as a pumpkin. And, strange to say, the elder wasn't hurt one mite, 'cept in his feelings. Oh, he was terrible riled. And, well, that minister said he laid his mortal salvation to the keel of providence.

Now, that boy's folks never did a thing to him except to laugh—hmmmm. There'd been something done besides laughing if he'd been a boy of mine.

Mrs. SARAH MAHON MALSBARY
MINNEAPOLIS, MINNESOTA

When I was born I was such a puny little thing. And they told me that when I was a few days old, my grandfather came in from the barn and said, "Isn't that poor little thing dead yet?"

My father was a Methodist preacher, and I was the oldest of five children. My brothers were considerably younger, so I did the boy's work. I did anything a boy would do around the place. There was nobody else to do it. And I used to go around with Father to the churches and take care of the horse for him. He preached at one place in the morning and another place in the afternoon and then at the home church in the evening, and so I always took care of the horse when he was preaching. One time I was waiting on him—he was talking to somebody in the church—and this man that was a friend of our family's said, "You needn't to wait on your father. I'll bring you home with me." So I went on to his house, and I found a stall in the stable and put Dolly up, and when they came out of their house, he said, "Where's your horse?" I said, "Well, I put her up and fed her." He said, "Did you go *behind* that bay mare of mine?" I said, "Well, there's no other way to get there." He said, "Well, it's a wonder you're not injured. She won't let anybody go behind her without seeing them first." I had a girlish belief of a guardian angel, so I just thought she'd taken care of me.

Now, we had Dolly for a long time. But we moved to a place where Father had no use for a horse, and it was too expensive to keep her, so Father wanted to find a good home for her. He finally found a lady who lived on a very small farm where Dolly would have plenty of outdoors and plenty of grass. He sold her to this woman—I forget her name now. She was a maiden lady. Shortly after he sold her, they began making a new road through where this lady lived.

And they needed horses to do the work—just the hardest, heaviest kind of work, hauling stone and things like that. And she sold our little horse to those people. We children had a time of rejoicing when we found out that Dolly was found dead in her stall the next morning. She couldn't have taken that work and the lady just wanted to make some money out of her.

The bad thing in my life is the man I married. It wasn't a love marriage; I felt sorry for him was all. I forget how I first met him, but at any rate he was telling me about what a hard time he had had. His father deserted his mother, and when his mother died his father married a young girl and went to California. And so on—a whole lot of stuff. And he had had such a hard time that when he asked me to marry him I thought, well—foolish youngster that I was—I'd give him a happy life.

Instead of that, he gave me the unhappiest life I'd ever dreamed of. And his own sister said, "Why don't you leave him?" And I said, "Well, how can I with five children?" Five children in nine years. He didn't care a cent for one of them. But, finally, I felt if I kept on living with him I'd be as bad as he was, and I left him.

But I was able to make a living. I was a good stenographer and I understood medical terms and very few stenographers then did, so I always had work.

Of the good things I don't know what to say excepting that I was a Christian. Well, that tells it all. I got a great deal of satisfaction out of my beliefs. I felt safe, and not very much disturbed me. Rather, it took a good deal to disturb me. I just felt that I was a Christian, that I was being taken care of.

That's my belief. And I think that everyone who is a real Christian—I mean in their beliefs—is happier than someone who has no belief. Now there's a man here that doesn't believe there's a God. He can't be happy.

Mr. W. C. GLACZIER
GULFPORT, MISSISSIPPI

The fastest changes I've seen during my life was our science when they elevated our eyes up with Sputnik, you know. Then the atomic bomb has made us bend our knees and supplicate a little bit—pray. It put the fear into people. It brought them back to realize that there is a power that can destroy them, see. But look at them now; they take it for granted. Those were two blessings that science blessed us with, see. They used to say, oh, science ain't helping us—yes, it is. Those are the two blessings that we had. Well, from then on, we progressed very rapidly in aviation—and in submarines, too, underwater. We had some submarines that went down mighty deep, whereas before that time we only could go just so far. And they hadn't yet attained a sound control for the submarines. But now they have it. Look at these airplanes, these jet planes, they have the air condition, the sound condition in there, where you don't get your eardrums busted or heart failure and all that. Just normal in there just like you were on the ground. And we're still progressing scientifically. We will eventually—I imagine within the next generation, even before 2000—we'll have big spaceships up in space. But they'll be assembled on some of these satellites, see, where they'll have piers, just like what we have for ships down here. . . . Pads, they'll call them pads up there. And they'll assemble these spaceships up there. This has to be done above the ground quite a ways because of the tremor and the thrust of these big jet spaceships. You understand we got some that have already attained 25,000 thrust power. You know that's a terrific power—30,000 miles an hour. They couldn't take off from the earth they'd cause so many earthquakes and whatnot. And then another thing—with the roar and the terrific jar of these planes taking off, there'd be houses shattered for miles away. So we know we can't take off from the earth. We have to have a pad up there on

one of these satellites. Now, when we're speaking of a satellite, we're not speaking of a little disc just about five or six hundred feet; it would probably be about . . . oh . . . 25,000. Because that would be a regular town up there. People will have to have rooming houses, hotels, barber shops, even schools, I imagine. This is my concept and my vision of what they'll have to do. It's possible. . . . Why, yes, there could be intelligent life on other planets. I'm entertaining a possibility. There might be subterranean life on the moon, you know. They haven't found anything on the surface, but there could be subterranean life there. I'm assuming my theory from these coal mines we have in Pennsylvania and Virginia. You know, at one time there were grown people working down there in those mines who were born down there and had never seen daylight. And the same thing could be on the moon. And, yes, I would like to be living when they find life on another planet. Because I'm curious about what kind of guttural sound we'd hear, whether they speak our language. But more likely they'd speak a Coptic version of sign language just like the Indians, see, which is the eldest knowledge of communication. Now, that I would expect. . . . Oh, we're advancing rapidly. Earlier in the century they thought it would be seventy-five years before we got any knowledge of atomic power. Then here we get Albert Einstein—he gives us relativity. With relativity we equate the quantum of life. Albert gave us that.

Mr. JOE TAYLOR
EATONTON, GEORGIA

I was born the second year of Freedom. That's when my father told me I was born. I just know my father's name. His name was Edmond Taylor. And my father before he died, he told me I was born the second year of Freedom. Now, you know that's a long time.

I stay here with my wife all the time. She's in the house. Her name is Matilda Taylor. She can't see. Me and her been together a long time. She stays with me. She can't see or talk much, but yet she's here with me. She keeps me company.

Mrs. ANNA McANDREW
ELLSWORTH, WISCONSIN

I taught school for ten years. I started teaching when I was sixteen. I wanted to start teaching when I was fifteen, and I took the examination and wrote the superintendent. And the superintendent wrote back; he said you passed, you had a good examination, but we're not allowed to give a certificate because I was only fifteen years of age. So he said you write again next year and I assure you that you can teach. You know, I was anxious to be a schoolteacher, so next year I wrote, I done just as he said. And I got a certificate and I commenced teaching in the higher grades. I taught school ten years, till I was married.

Oh, I always had a good time teaching school. I was always lonesome when my school was out. I always had nice children. Once or twice I've had a little trouble in school, but very seldom. There are always a couple of discordant ones. You can't expect them all to be good, you know. If I got mad and told 'em what I thought, they'd never do the thing over again. I didn't give 'em a licking the first time, I just shook 'em up a little bit. They knew I was boss, so they minded.

One time I had a little boy, he didn't belong in our district, but he got kind of in love with me and he wanted to come to our school. So one day I was in geography class, and I had a geography book in my hand, and I was standing up to tell something to some of the children. And this little boy, he looks at me, and he walked over and he began to nudge me and pudge me. Kind of molest me, you know. I didn't say a word, I just turned around, and I gave him a whack on the head with the geography book. He was so startled he didn't know what to do. I was frightened after I did it. I didn't think I was sending him such a hard blow when I knocked him. He got up, got in his seat. But he never liked me after that. I had to show him I was boss.

You got to be boss or you can't do anything. I don't mean to be mean, but you just gotta let 'em know that you're the one that's the boss.

What makes you happy?

Nothing in particular. Because I can't see, I can't read. I get letters from my friends, and I can't read them. I have to wait for someone to come and read them to me. Mrs. Jack Riley was my best friend, and she died in her sleep.

Who's your best friend?

I ain't got any now. Mrs. Jack Riley was my best friend, and she died in her sleep. She died in her sleep. I got up in the morning and told 'em something I wanted to tell Mrs. Riley. I said, "You tell her for me." Why, they said—they looked so funny—they said, "Mrs. Riley isn't here anymore." I said, "She isn't here? Where is she?" They said, "She's dead." It was just a terrible shock to me. We lived together, I had a room in her house. She was well liked, very well loved. She died in her sleep.

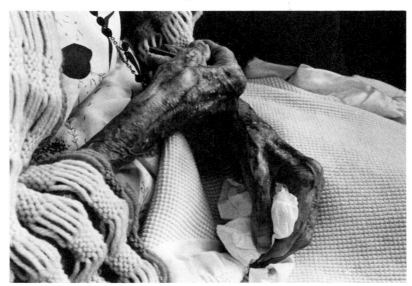

❧ 104 ❧

Mr. PETER NELSEN
MASON CITY, IOWA

I was born in Denmark. Over there when I got to be fifteen, sixteen years old, if a farmer wanted a big kid to herd cows and sheep or something like that, he'd come over and ask my mother and my father if he could have me for a few days or a week and so on. And I'd go over there and get my room and board and get a few crowns, you know. I did that up until I got to be about eighteen, then I hired out, you know, as a hired man on the farm. Then when I got twenty years old I went in the Army, stayed in a couple of years.

Well, I didn't have no chance a'tall in Denmark. You know, my father wasn't well-fixed . . . of course he was well-fixed to his way of thinking, but for us children we wanted to get something for ourself. So I came to America.

I didn't know nobody when I landed in this country. I came over by my own self. But I felt all right. I was young, and I didn't give a care what. And I didn't care what kind of work I got into.

This feller in New York had kind of a cave underground, a place under the streets, where he had everything you raise in the summertime, had everything from roots and potatoes up through cabbage and carrots and such a thing. And he had three wagons, by God, that went there in New York and peddled them roots, potatoes, cabbage, and all sorts of things. I got a job down there to sort them and see that they wasn't spoiled. And the feller I worked for, he liked to talk to me, because I couldn't understand him and he couldn't understand me. I didn't speak no English when I came here. Oh, I'd heard sailors from England or somewhere place that come into the ports in Denmark—they could swear. Yep, that's all the English I knew. . . . Well, anyway, I worked there for a little while, but I didn't like it. Being down there in the dark. Sitting underground. So after I got a little of this here American money, I told him I quit.

67

Where I lived, there was another fellow there, another Dane. He could talk English. And we went up to a small town in New York; they made bricks by the millions every day. We'd wheel 120 at one time and not tip 'em over and spoil 'em. When you got used to it, you could easy manage it.

Well, after a while, I quit there and went to New Jersey. That was better there, and we'd make them fancy bricks. They used to in olden times—I don't know what they do now, but back then when they put up apartments or big skyscrapers, oh, they used all kinds of fancy bricks with designs. That's a good job. Sit there and pound with a little hammer and a chisel, making the designs on the brick. Nothing to that, after you get into it.

And then I got to traveling. Got tired of every goddamn thing and thought I would go to some other state. I traveled around from the harvest fields in Dakota and down to the orange picking in Texas. Chaffed wheat and barley, by gosh, from Jersey state clear out to California. I've seen enough of the country in my young days.

We were two of us traveling, me and Curley. We rode in these here side-door sleepers—boxcars on a freight train. Sometimes we stood on the bumper between the engine and the baggage car. Get an idea into you that you don't like a place, all you need to do is go up to the railroad station and wait for a train. I've helped the fireman a good many nights and even days, if the engineer wasn't a crank. Sometimes the engineer wouldn't say a word and the fireman, he was glad to have some help. Oh, I fired railroads!

Oh, yes, we had good times. But sometimes it was so bad the marshal was out for us. He'd say, "If you don't leave town, I'll put you in." "Got any money?" Told him, "We have a few dollars. And we'll hold onto it so you don't take it." I did get locked up two times. One time Curley and me were standing in front of a big restaurant, on our way to South Dakota. Someone tapped me on the shoulder. I looked around to see who it was, and it was a policeman. I said, "I'm on my way out of town." And he says, "Not for a while. I know you." So I said, "Well, you don't know me for anything bad or anything good. You never saw me before. And, by God, if you don't take your dirty hands off me, one officer will go down." And, by God, they put me in jail . . . and closed the door.

I sat there till two o'clock, and then the judge wanted to see me. And this policeman took me up there to the courtroom. The judge shook his head and asked where I come from, and I told him—told him a lie of course. And where was I going? "I'm going to South Dakota. We just got off the train, and this cop here put me in jail." "It must have been a mistake," he said. So I got out. I don't know what I was arrested for. Someone had done something and I was looking like him; I don't know.

Me and Curley, we always had, oh, not a lot of money, but anyhow enough to get by on. I had lots of different jobs. You see, I was never anything but a common laborer. Of course, I wasn't afraid to tackle anything. Oh, heck no. Well, the job I liked best, that was when I was a streetcar motorman. That was in Omaha, Nebraska. You stayed out there by yourself in the fresh air in the front. All you need to do is just push that brake handle, and she'd stop. I liked that one, by God!

Well, I got tired of roaming. So I started working on farms around Omaha. And then I got married and stayed married for forty-nine years. When I met her, she was working on a neighboring farm as a hired girl. I went over to the neighbors a good many times. And, by God, some way or another we got to know each other. And in them days, you know, we rode around in a horse and buggy, Satur-

day nights or Sunday. We didn't do nothing we shouldn't done, I'll admit that. So I met her, and we decided to get married. We did.

Well, I had a little money saved up. I had worked on farms. Went to town and spent most of it for beer and other drinks, but I saved a little. Me and my wife got to talking about how we'd like to live on a farm, if I could rent a farm. So I borrowed some money from the bank and rented a farm and I did pretty goddamn well. Always kept good horses and some cattle. And then we got a goddurn cyclone. Oh, my God, it cleaned us out. Horses and cattle and everything I had was killed. And then we got in these here poor times. By God, you couldn't do nothing on the farm. So we had to go to town, and I got a job at a nursery, and I worked there for fifteen or sixteen years.

Yep, I've had lots of good luck and lots of bad luck. I had a little black team once, a goddamn nice looking team, and I had raised 'em myself from the colts. I broke 'em and worked 'em right along. They got to be five years old. And in the spring of one year, they was out in the yard, playing like they was colts. This fellow was driving by on the road where I lived, the Number 3 Highway, and he drove in there, and he sit and talked to me while I stood out in the yard. Finally, he said, "You got a nice pair of horses out there." "You wouldn't take $300 for 'em would you?" And I says, "No." "Well," he says, "if I offered you $350?" "No," I say, "not if you offered me four." "Well," he said, "I can't buy 'em, but I'd like to have 'em." And the day after, on an Easter Sunday, we were out in the yard, and the colts were out there playing. And then it started in with some awful thundering and lightning, and they started coming home in a gallop. And the lightning struck down the fence they were running along and killed both of 'em. Yep. But, my God, I was tough in them days. And I could have just about cried.

Yep, I've seen a lot. And now I've landed here in this Odd Fellows Home. I've been here eighteen, twenty years. It's all right, goddammit, I had a good time here. Up till they put me on the sawing block and sawed that leg off, about a year and a half ago. And then after it healed up and got so I could get around, they tried to learn me to walk on the one leg and a crutch. Why, you may as well have killed a rabbit, catch it by the tail. I couldn't learn it. You can't do nothing alone, you can't do *nothing* alone.

No . . . I've seen enough and tried enough. . . .

Mrs. EMILY HARTSHORN
MONT VERNON, NEW HAMPSHIRE

Mrs. Hartshorn still lives in the same big white house on a hill in which she was born. She says she likes having lived in the same place all her life, "but of course all of my old friends are gone." The diminutive lady, who did not marry until her fifties, was a school-teacher. She taught fifth grade for forty years at the same school, and her former pupils still come to visit her.

Yes, I've seen a lot of changes, and there's one that I don't want to see. They're building a new development here in Mont Vernon. Just spoiling things. That's been a beautiful view. But this man bought it and sold it to the developers, called it progress. And I don't think it is, because it'll be laid out into streets and houses built and nobody knows what kind of people. Anything for money! You have to have some, but it's too bad to spoil places.

Rev. BOB BROOKS
WARNER ROBBINS, GEORGIA

In 1865 the bell rung from the North to the South Pacific that the colored people won't be slaves no more. It was the thirtieth of May and I was going on twelve years old. The bell rung. The news got out—from North to South, East to West, across the Mason-Dixon line clean back down here to this place Cuba—that the colored people won't be slaves no more. And the flag of peace was held. The war stopped.

We weren't doing anything but playing. And that day when the bell rung, the white ladies was walking about crying with the babies in their arms. "The niggers are free and how are we gonna manage now? How are we gonna set up a standard?" The white man said, "Hush, wife, we will see how conditions will be."

Back then they had a trough out in the yard for we colored children. We ate out of a trough. It was some kind of poplar tree, and they went in the woods and got it. And had wooden spoons for us to eat jungle bread crumbled up in milk. And we sat there and talked. They had slats across the trough like in a hog pen where I couldn't meddle over in your part and you couldn't meddle in mine. They had old women, from fifty to sixty years old, to tend to we colored children.

At that time I was glad to get food from anywhere. We didn't have people to talk to us like they're talking to the children now, people to advise us what not to do and how to do and all like that. About once a month we got a biscuit from my missus. And they had molasses syrup. They give us all a biscuit that certain Sunday morning. Well, I'd take that biscuit and set it over there in that black syrup— looked like mule blood. And I'd lick that biscuit and put it back in my bosom. I wouldn't eat that biscuit right away. I'd save that biscuit, take it out sometimes when I'd be out in the yard playing hiding sticks and take a bite from it.

The white ladies along in then was so particular that when they got to church, they didn't get out and get on the ground. General Rudleford and old generals in the war, captains and lieutenants and sergeants in the war—their daughters was so rich they didn't get out and put their foots on the ground. They had that driver drive on up there to the doorsteps of the church and them daughters would walk off of the steps of the chariot onto the steps of the church.

I know what to tell you. But the thing about your tongue is sometimes it will stop you from eating bread. There is a time to talk, time to laugh and then there's a time to weep and cry—over conditions. My wife kept telling me that y'all were coming here from Atlanta, and the views of my mind got wide open just like you

throw open a door. I getting ready and prepared to meet you. I had confidence in you to come to catch my voice. And some of it I have better sense than to put it out. There are some things you must talk about, and some things you must let alone. We have peace and harmony. You look how close the things have done got together now. You sitting here on this porch without any fear or without being uneasy. And there's a different color in here—white and black is sitting here together. There have been a time that we couldn't do this. We used to have chariots that would go up to your door. The man driving the chariot would be up there, and the passenger was down inside. And what the passenger said, the driver would hand it down to the master. Now what I'm telling you today, it's worth a millions of dollars to the world.

Now when I first went to Macon, I had no mother and no father, and everywhere the people would treat me good—I'd put up there to stay. Long as I could. And when I first went to Macon I went from down here on 41—wasn't no 41 then, just a dirt road—and I went from there to Macon. There wasn't nothing there but an old Southern car shed and the old Southland Hotel. Mr. Macon lived over there across the river. That's the man that cut the jungles out—the rat canyons, grapevines and bamboos—and shot up houses there —Mr. Macon. And he lived over on the other side of the river in a log cabin, it was about forty or fifty feet long.

My mother fell and cracked her skull when I was six years old. Cooking on a stove for the mistress in the days of slavery. And the blood rushed to her head, and they didn't know nothing about high blood then and heart failure then. They didn't know nothing except about consumption. She fell and cracked her skull and died when I was six years old, and my father left me when I was seven. And I didn't lay my eyes on him again until all my children was grown. First one and then another raised me. White folks, black folks, and I stayed with an old Indian woman.

The chief of police's grandmother let me go to school. I was staying with her. White folks had been teaching me in their homes, but I hadn't never been to no school. And I only went to school one day, and the chief of police's grandmother let me go to school. I was out in the yard chopping stove wood. It was cold, and all the children were walking to school. She put her head out the window and she

said, "Bob, you want to go to school, don't you?" I said, "Yes'm."
So she put some cornbread and peas in a bucket and put a piece of
paper over it. And she said, "This food is for you to eat at recess."
So I went that day, and they had a spelling bee, and they was giving
a twenty-five-cent bunch of candy canes for a prize. I was standing
up there in my shirttails; all the other children had on pants. And
everybody would have to spell a word, and if they couldn't spell it
they would have to go to their place to sit down. Till finally I sat 'em

all down. I got the candy, and the children wanted a piece. Then the teacher said, "You better save some of that candy to show to your mother for what you have done." He said, "Who is your mother?" I said, "I ain't got no mother." He said, "Who is your father?" "I ain't got no father."

I was going on fifteen years old before I put on a pair of pants. I wore a red oak shirt when I was a little old boy and had a little split up under my arms. And I was sixteen before I put on a pair of shoes. I seen the time I put my feet on the floor and the blood would ooze out of my heels and toes from being frostbitten. And I seen the time when snow would stay on the backside of the house, behind the barn, two or three months after it quit snowing. It don't snow here no more like it used to. The wind don't blow like it used to. There ain't no more food like there used to be. There ain't no control of children. They in the streets. Their mother birth 'em, but they ain't got time to raise 'em. They sucklin' 'em on all kinds of milk. It could be dog or mule or horse or some kind of milk. And the children now, the sun almost never shine on 'em. Because ain't nobody got time to raise the children. There ain't but a few people now giving the children a prayer down at the bedside at night. They ain't doing nothing like that, they ain't got *time*. Everybody in a hurry—got to go. Women ain't got time now to make a whole dress—they cutting 'em off way long up here. I been to the bottom of Florida and every-where preaching, and I'll be sitting up in the pulpit, and they all sitting out there in front of me, and I had to turn my back on the congregation. The women sit there and keep a pulling at these dresses and crossing their legs and all like that, and I knowed what it was all about.

Everybody now wanna move to town and don't wanna work for a living. They ain't nothing but a midnight rambler. A gambler, a pool player, and a poker player. There used to be a time thirty-five men would be plowing mules in the fields but now they ain't got but one tractor. And back across the river white ladies tie up their dresses and get on the tractors. Nobody wants to work no more. Nobody wants to raise food. Butterbeans, turnip greens, sweet pota-toes. It's under there, but they don't wanna suffer to get it, work to get it. Don't wanna get dusty. Peoples ought to think about the long suffering that they had.

There didn't used to be no storms like there is now. Storms were so seldom, and the people was uneasy, they'd sit down and read the Bible and see where the Bible say the time *would* come when there would be earthquakes and storms and tornadoes and all like that. But it would come from disobedience! If the people would be more sensitive about paying their just and honest debts! The preacher in the church and in the pulpit, he telling the people what to do, how come *he* don't do it? Need more God-name users in the world. Jehovah, that's the chief cornerstone.

Ain't nobody gone to the moon. Ain't nothing but a racket. The moon governs the night. The moon controls nature. Nothing favors the moon except a woman. The moon goes through thirteen changes in a year, and the women go through thirteen changes. The moon is supposed to be made in blood. It's not like a He-thing. A man can't favor the moon. Nothing on earth is born except by the leadership of the moon.

Now I done found out. Right there in Florida when the missile went to rise to shoot up, lightning struck it. When Noah's son built that tower, they was gonna walk to heaven. And when they called for mortar, they would send bricks. And when they called for bricks, they sent mortar. God done changed their language. And when they got high enough to see the wonders of Zion, God tore down that thing and scattered 'em to the four corners of the earth.

Yessir, and I'm the father of forty-two children by three wives. And I've got over a hundred grand- and eighty or ninety great-grand- and fifty or fifty-five great-great grandchildren. And they all know me. They come here to see me from Florida and California and all about. They send me greetings. Now, tomorrow is Father's Day. And I get more greetings, cards, envelopes, with a dollar in it, sometimes five dollars. Well, if I don't never see you no more I've got room enough in my heart to dry my lips and kiss the paper; tell God I'm much obliged to Him.

Mr. FRANK MIGNAULT
FRAMINGHAM, MASSACHUSETTS

I'll tell you, a lot of people ask me where I get my longevity. And one man said the other day, "Your walking is what did it. That's why you're 100." I lived in East Boston when I was a kid. And of course you know as well as I do that there was nothing then; nothing to do, no autos, no pictures of any kind or anything like that—nothing! So we had to do something. You know little kids have got to get out. They can't stay in the house, sit in the chair and fold their hands— they want to get out.

So all there was to do was to walk. And every night after supper we used to go over to Chelsea from East Boston. We used to walk up Bennington Street to Central Square, that was only about two blocks. Then we'd walk up Meridian Street toward Chelsea. And that was quite a little walk to Chelsea Bridge. Across Chelsea Bridge. Then we'd take a left and get down to Broadway, Chelsea, and go way up Broadway and back. That round trip is a good four miles. Every night. Well, that's the way it was done.

So I think myself walking is the best thing you can do. Especially when you're a kid. Why, a kid nowadays only walks about a hundred feet and he wants to get in a car. He doesn't want to walk a'tall. That's bad. I think it's bad, anyway.

East Boston. I lived there seventeen years. Grew up there. 'Cause I remember well my mother died the year . . . before my birthday, I think it was, before my seventeenth birthday. She had pneumonia. And the doctor didn't know how to cure it then. Well, that was my mother. She always baked a cake for me for my birthday, but I can remember her saying, "I can't bake a cake for you this year." Pretty sad, isn't it?

83

I worked for Denison forty-five years. I was the paymaster. I handled some money there—yes, quite a lot of money—more than I'm handling it now. I got out of there in '46. I haven't earned a dollar in twenty-six years. Not a dollar.

My wife died about sixteen years ago, and I lived in my house alone for fifteen years. It wasn't too bad—of course it was lonesome. I'd have to talk to myself some. Ask questions and never get the answers.

Mrs. ALICE OTTO
MOUND, MINNESOTA

One hundred years, that's a long time to live.

Yes, it is. Too long for some people. I'm getting pretty tired of it, I'll tell you. Sitting here. Can't go out, you know. But we have a lot of company and so that helps while away the time.

You must have seen a lot of changes in your life.

Oh, mercy! From ox teams to automobiles. I know when I was a little girl, we used to go berrying quite a lot with my grandmother, and when she'd sit down to eat her lunch she'd tell us tales, you know. One time she told us about horseless carriages and flying ships. And we thought she was crazy.

What are the biggest changes you've seen?

We didn't have the murdering or the suicides or the snowmobiles in those days. The snowmobiles are killing all the people.

I think of things farther back better than I do of the present. My memory's better about things back then. My father, he worked in the woods, you know, and drove down the Mississippi with the logs in the spring. When they'd come down the river, I remember we'd go there and get good cats. They'd take us there and feed us, you know. Oh, that was a long time ago. And I've far forgotten, really forgotten. It's hard for me to tell anything and tell it right.

I had a wonderful husband. A wonderful family. We never knew what it was to have liquor or anything like that in the house. And I never allowed them to gamble or play cards on Sunday. I had eight children. I lost one in infancy out in Wyoming. My other two sons died here. They are both buried in Minnesota, and one is buried in Wyoming.

I was my husband's second wife. He and his first wife, wherever they went, they used to take me with 'em. She died of typhoid fever, buried in April. And five years later he and I got married. I couldn't say no to him hardly. Well, I knew him, I knew who I was getting, I knew I wasn't getting an alcoholic or anything.

Yes, I had a wonderful married life. I've been a widow an awful long time. He died in '39 I think. Thirty-three years of a lonesome life, I'll tell you. Since he's died it's been lonesome. I never seen anybody I ever thought could take his place. Never. But I thought I had a nice family. They were all nice children. So I have no complaints.

The only complaint I have is living here alone—without my husband. My daughter waiting on me and I can't do nothing to help her back in return.

I bet you keep her company sometimes.

Oh, I don't know whether I do or not. Sometimes I wonder.

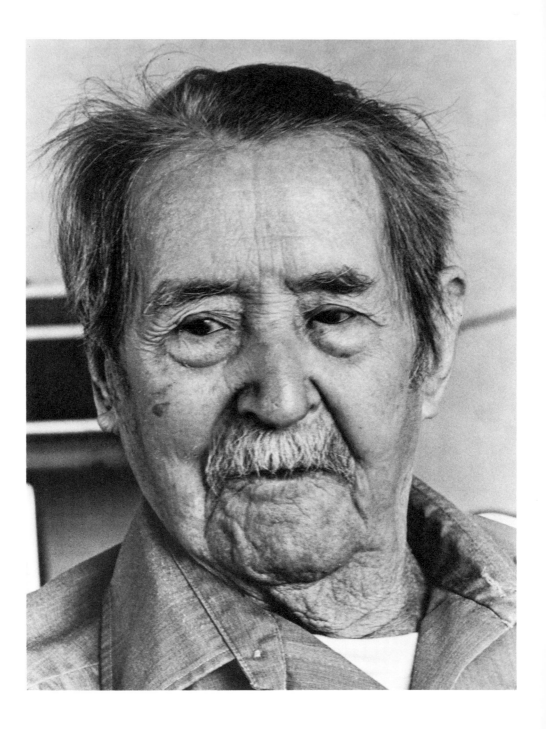

Mr. NELS NELSON
FRANKLIN, MASSACHUSETTS

I've been lucky all my life. Ever since I left home. I'm an old Swede-head, born in Sweden, and I left home when I was just a kid. And I've had a pretty good time. Saturday nights and Sundays, go to a pub, something like that. But now I've run downhill.

I love every man and girl I ever knew. Haven't thought anything hard against them.

I can't remember things now. I can't tell anybody anything now because I'm just too old to do it. I don't know how much longer I'm going to be able to get around.

Saturday nights and Sundays we played games, you know. Played poker. Now all I can do is eat a little and go to bed.

I call myself lucky. I very rarely have to ask anybody for anything. I've always been healthy. Always free to go where I want to, do what I want to. And I used to have a lot of fun. Saturday nights and Sundays, play games, sip a little beer to go with it. But them days are over for me now.

My time is gone.

Mrs. RUFINA NAVE
NORRISTOWN, PENNSYLVANIA

Mrs. Nave's granddaughter talks about the oldest member of her family:

She lived on a farm in Italy. She was eighteen when she married her husband. She was forty-three when he died and left her to rear the children. She had to rear eleven children—seven children actually, all the others died. The children were all small when her husband died; the youngest was three years old. And she worked on the farm and raised all the kids. They all used to follow her while she was out on the farm, digging and planting.

She came to this country eighteen years ago, and last week she became the oldest person ever to be naturalized a citizen of the United States. And she knocked a guy on his back in the courthouse the day she got her citizenship. He was a TV cameraman, and he was kneeling down to film her, and she gave him a whack and knocked him on his back because she thought he was trying to look up her dress.

Mrs. Nave: What's passed will never be back again. My past—that won't be back again. There are things you should forget, once in the past. Today, I am very pleased that most of the family live on the same street.

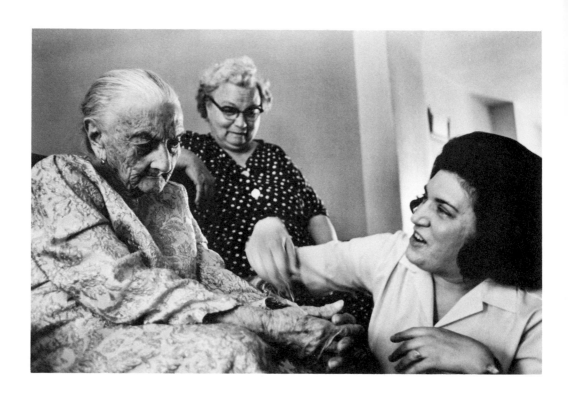

Mr. THOMAS ANDERSON
NINETY-SIX, SOUTH CAROLINA

As a young man, I became a surveyor. My father was a doctor, but he utilized surveying on the plantation, and he taught me surveying before I ever went to college. And I knew a good deal about it before I even went to college. In fact, I believe I knew a good deal more about it than a lot of the college graduates. I had had so much experience and so much good teaching that I was pretty well equipped when I first went to school.

And I didn't stay in college very long because I was a good plow hand and Daddy couldn't spare me. If I hadn't plowed so well, he probably would have let me go to school. But his will was law in those days. He liked to be obeyed and demanded respect and obedience. So I had to stay home and plow.

That was right after the Civil War, and you can im . . . —I started to say you can imagine, but you can't. You can't imagine what we went through right after the Civil War. But I'll never forget it. You see, I was born in '68. Well, that was just three years after Surrender. The South was prostrate. Many of the best soldiers had been killed in the war, lost their lives in the war. And all their property you might say was destroyed, because their slaves were set free.

When the slaves were freed, my daddy called up what few he had on his plantation there and says, "Well, you're free now. You can leave if you wish." But they didn't have any place to go. They didn't have a home. They didn't have any land. And they were legally free, but they were not really free. Don't you see? They were bound by the circumstances of nature. They were compelled to stay. Well, I don't think they ever wanted to go. But it was almost a disgrace to know how some of the landholders treated their slaves after Freedom, how they exploited their labor. Worked them as hard as mules, and they wasn't feeding 'em hardly nothing. Well, you might say the landholders didn't have anything; some of the farmers had lost almost all they had. That was true, but that don't excuse 'em. That don't excuse 'em.

So most of my father's field hands stayed on the place—they had to stay. Had cabins that they lived in. A big fireplace where they cooked their meals on a hearth—didn't have any stove. As a matter of fact my mother herself—before they had a stove—cooked at this house in the yard that had a crane that came out and held the pot over the fire. And what they called a bread hole where they cooked the biscuits. I could almost stand up in the fireplace, and you could take a stick of cordwood four feet long and put on the fire. I don't know why I didn't save some of those old things. I wish I had . . .

Well, anyway, as a boy about ten years old, my father's rule was to let me go out on Monday, Monday at noon, and all the field hands were called up, and I issued 'em rations. What you reckon I gave 'em for a weekly supply? Everything I gave 'em had been raised on the farm. I had a peck measure, and I gave 'em a peck of meal, and we made our own sorghum syrup—we had a mill that could make a fine quality syrup—a peck of meal, a quart of syrup, two pounds of bacon—homemade bacon—and sometimes ten or fifteen pounds of flour, what they called cake bread. I'm afraid they had to pay for that cake bread because it didn't come in a regular ration too often. "We can't eat meal and bacon all through the week! Got to have some cake bread." And they ought to have had it. So those poor darkies had to take that stuff and cook it themselves on the hearth. When the men caught the mules out at sunrise to go plowing, their wives stayed at home, cooked their breakfast, put it in a bucket and took it to the fields. And they sat down on the plowstock and ate their breakfast.

Yessir, I played with some of the field hand's children. In those days those old farmers lived far apart and transportation was not very good. All the mules and horses had to work on the farm. Except my father kept a buggy horse. But the children were not often allowed to use it, except on special occasions. That reminds me of a right interesting story.

I was about eight years old. That was the time of the Red Shirts. Threw off the carpetbagger yoke in South Carolina. Those Yankees came down here, you know, got the darkies in the capital in Colum-

bia, run the white folks out. And we were determined to get possession of our capital and our government again, and they organized companies of Red Shirts. The only uniform was the red shirt. Well, they were very proud of their Red Shirt brigade. My two brothers belonged to it; I wasn't old enough. And one day they were going to have a big celebration down at the old Star Fort—I wish I had time to go down there now. They were going to have an all-day picnic and a speaker and a prize for the best drills. I can remember my brother at the old home place going through the manual of arms. "Right shoulder arms! Present arms!" and all that sort of thing. I don't know where he ever got the knowledge—I don't think he did.

But, anyway, my older brother George had married a girl just across the creek. Old Mr. Brooks, a right wealthy old Baptist man, had two right pretty granddaughters. One of 'em had red hair, and she was very intelligent. And my older brother went over there, courted her and married her, and he had red hair. Well, the day of the Red Shirt celebration my younger brother hitched up the gray mule and ran over there to my older brother George, who was married to the red-headed girl. And my younger brother told him, "I wanna get your good horse and buggy you got when you married. I don't wanna drive my girl with a gray mule." So George let him have the horse and buggy, and me and George rode in a buggy with the gray mule.

So we started down for the old Star Fort for the big celebration, with me and George and the gray mule in back of my other brother that had the horse. And we were jogging on down the road, we weren't going real fast, the gray mule trying to catch up with the horse. You don't know how those old mules sometimes get attached to the horses. And my older brother got out to arrange something about the bridle; we stopped just for a moment on top of a hill sorta. And the other buggy kept on, they didn't look behind. Well, my brother very carelessly threw the reins across the dashboard. And while he was working on the bridle the old gray mule took a notion to catch up with that horse—she was *foolish* about the horse. And off she went, dik, dik, dik, dik, just as hard as she could go. And me sitting there. I didn't even have the reins in my hands. We didn't go very far before the front wheel of the buggy hit a big rock on the side of the road. And out we went, me and the rifle. We had the

rifle they practiced drills with sitting under the buggy seat. And that buggy wheel hit my leg. The mule went on and she stopped when she caught up with the horse. My oldest brother had to catch her and bring her back, and they put me back in the buggy, picked up the rifle, and we went on to the celebration.

Well, they didn't know my leg was broken but it was. Old Dr. Maxwell from Greenwood examined my leg. They didn't have any way to examine it in those days, so he put his ear down to my leg, and he started to shake those bones to see if it was broken. He raised his head up and said, "Well, I don't think it's broken." Well, that was a relief to my brothers. So they left me there all day on the ground with my leg on a pillow; didn't know it was broken. And had their drill contest for the Red Shirts. I don't know who got the prize.

Do you think people are any different now from when you were a child?

Not naturally. Not naturally. But they have a different training. They are not coming up under the same circumstances. That's where the trouble is. The children have not the chance to go through the discipline and the training that they used to have. When they used to grow up on the farm and lived in a family group, it was quite different. You know that, don't you? You can see it. Conditions are so different, unfortunately, that we haven't the opportunity to teach our children as we used to. Lot of the mothers and fathers working in industrial plants. That's the main trouble. There's not the opportunity of family unity, family training, family love and devotion. I don't know what's going to solve it, what's going to be the outcome. We live in times that are changing so fast that we can't predict what's going to happen.

It's astonishing how quick these young people have come up now. They don't remember anything about the Civil War or the Reconstruction, what we went through with. And there's not much you should tell them, because they don't understand it. They can't take it in.

In those days the poor farmers—what we call the dirt farmers— the sharecroppers, they didn't own any land much, and made their living from picking cotton and pulling fodder and working in the fields. And for seventy-five cents a day. Working hard and getting scarcely enough to live on. Some people moved out from a town down here called Kirksey, came up to Greenwood and built a cotton mill and a bank and started an enterprise. And those old sharecroppers were glad to come up here to Greenwood and work for a dollar a day at first. But they gave 'em a place to live, and they didn't have a house fit to live in at home. They were good, honest people. And they stayed there and prospered.

On the railroads labor was cheap and everything was done by hand. And the laborers got paid more than on the farm. And they were glad, of course, that just a few of 'em could get a place to work on the railroad. I remember one of my father's field hands used to say he was gonna try to get a job working on the railroad. Each boss had about eight miles of track he kept up. But now you don't find the man that works on the railroad; they have machinery that come along and do it.

Now we have just about one freight train a day, one up and one down, hauling pulpwood. All the passenger trains are stopped on this route like they have on most of the others. And the old telegraph wires are down. And I hate to see the old locomotive go, the beautiful steam locomotive. That old steam locomotive was a beautiful piece of machinery. Now they have an electric driven unit there that's all closed up and looks like an old tiger going along the road. I don't see anything pretty about it. But the old locomotive, it was a delight to see that old engine. Beautiful.

Mrs. LINDA RACEY

EDINA, MINNESOTA

I'll answer your questions if I can, but there's some I don't want to tell.

I was born in 1869 in southeastern Ohio on a farm. I lived on a farm. My father was one of these advanced farmers. He didn't have a very big farm; it was only 115 acres. But he'd read all he could about good farming, and we had one of the best equipped farms of anyone around there.

Growing up on a farm you had a sense of security—when a child is born in a place and raised there. Why, the farm had been in the family for twenty or more years. They took it up from a government claim, you know. Our farm was taken up under Monroe's administration. And the whole family was raised there, and when they'd marry off, why, they'd move maybe about a half a mile away. It would give you a sense of belonging there. Security, that's what you feel. And on each side of us about two or three miles away there was a church of the same denomination. I'd ride to church on my horse, and there was other young people, and I'd gather up somebody else on my way to church. They'd be riding too. I don't know, you just felt like they were a part of the family, you know, growing up with them from schooldays on. We'd go to the same school, same church and everything. You got so you felt like you belonged. You didn't know any other life.

Not very long ago I got a letter from a woman, and she seemed to know so much about me. She wrote as though she knew me. Well, I knew as soon as I opened the letter and started to read that I didn't know her from Adam. And I found out by reading her letter that I had married and left that neighborhood about the time she was born. She grew up after I had left. But, of course, living among my family she felt she knew me. I must have been a pretty lively one because she talked about me as though she thought she knew me.

Well, I was a lively one. I loved the horses. I didn't let my father know it because I didn't think he would like it, but I'd go down to the pasture field, take my saddle and carry it over my back by one stirrup. Then I'd sneak the bridle off one horse and on to another. I'd break the colts that way. So finally one day my father was out somewhere, and my sister came over—she was married—and she was riding one of these little Arabian horses. And I got on a colt that I had been breaking, but wasn't well broken. Had to go to the store, it was about two miles and a half. So when my sister went in the store I told her I wouldn't bother to get off Bonnie. And while I was sitting on the colt and trying to keep her quiet, why, here come my father. He looked at it and he looked at me and he says, "That's Bonnie, isn't it?" I says, "Yes." And he says, "Well, be careful." That's all he said. I thought I would be in for a lecture.

In those days I was always a great ham when the men gathered around the fire winter evenings. As they would gather around, I would often listen to 'em, talk to 'em. I know one winter I must have been only about four or five years old because it's about the first memory I have of people. And my father, I never sat on his lap, he never seemed to want me. But that winter, why, there was an old bachelor, he lived in with the family, he was a farm hand. And he would always sit with his chair leaned up against the wall—you've seen 'em do that. And he'd get all settled down right beside the fire, and then he'd put his arm down thataway, meant he wanted me to come over and get on his lap. Now, I never remember being on my father's lap—he didn't seem to like it. And this old man, he'd get me up there on his lap, and he'd teach me all kinds of little tricks with his hands and, oh, we'd have a good time for the evening.

When I got married, I left the whole neighborhood. I went to a small county seat about ten or twelve miles away, and then I went up into the city, I think Columbus. I was a good ways away from where I was raised. I didn't like leaving very well. I had to give up my colt that I'd broken and my riding horse. He was all black with a star right in the middle of his forehead. He and I got along wonderful. He knew what I was like, he liked me. So he never threw me.

My husband was a photographer. First time I ever saw him, my

oldest brother had some kind of party, and he was there. Took a group picture of 'em, and I got acquainted with him. We moved from the country into the cities, and my husband being a photographer we'd be around the galleries. For a while he ran a gallery. But he finally got kind of worthless. He wasn't much of a man. I raised three children, and when I was left alone I worshipped my children. If it hadn't been for my children I don't think I would have wanted to live.

I never make plans. I take life as it comes. I enjoy it more that way.

Miss ANNIE MARTIN
LAWRENCE, MASSACHUSETTS

I was born in Lawrence. I've lived here all my life. I was born on Concord Street. My mother and father was married in the Immaculate Conception Church. And I was baptized in that church.

My mother died when I was sixteen years old, and I was the oldest of seven children. And I stayed at home and helped to take care of the younger children, with my father. That was my life.

I took up sewing, and I made my living that way. I was a dressmaker. I made suits and coats and dresses. I sold the clothes I made right in the neighborhood and had the same customers all the time. I worked in my own home. My own home—my father owned it. Belonged to my father, it was left to me. I lived there until I came to this nursing home. And it still remains there.

How did you feel about having to stay home and take care of the other children?

I was satisfied with my life. I had a good healthy life, and they had a good home there, and I made myself acquainted with it. I was satisfied with that life. I was quite satisfied with it. I took in sewing in my spare time, and I made a living that way. It was my father's home, and I stayed home all the time. That was my life.

What makes you feel happy?

That I have good health. And I thank the Lord for it. I feel happy because I have good health. I trust in the Good Lord for my health. And I hope the Lord will continue it while I live. I trust He will.

Mrs. MAUDE CHAPMAN
MOUND, MINNESOTA

Mrs. Alice Cole, eighty-one years old, talks about her mother, who lives with her:

We thought she was wonderful. Of course, she was a hard worker. But she was full of fun, too. When my father was living she used to go to dances. She loved to dance. But, of course, she didn't go much after he died. I was five years old when he died and my brother was two. She was just a young woman, twenty-six years old, when he died. She raised us. We lived on a farm. Of course, she didn't do much of the farm work, only take care of the cattle. But she rented the farm out.

Her memory was better when she was 100 than it is now. She remembered the old times better. She's getting weaker now. She was able to get around quite well when she was 100. She would walk around the yard and look at the flowers and wash the dishes and cook breakfast if she got up before me. She enjoyed that. Now she doesn't act as though she enjoys anything in particular.

No, I'll tell you, she does enjoy her great-grandchildren. She has quite a few of 'em—thirteen. When they come to see her, she's happy. She's real happy then. She's all smiles and she talks to them.

Yes, I think she's a wonderful mother. She's been so good to me; she took such good care of us when we were children. And even after all these years and me taking care of her, I'll miss her terribly when she's gone. That is, if she goes before I do. She said one time she didn't want to live to bury her children. But she's buried one of us, and she was afraid she was going to have to bury me this time. But . . . she may outlive me.

Mrs. ELLA TAYLOR
RIVER FALLS, WISCONSIN

I was born near Barabou, Wisconsin, on a farm—on my grandfather's place. My father was a Methodist preacher; he commenced
preaching when he was eighteen. Until I was married, I was a
minister's daughter. And then after I married, I married a farmer.

We farmed in the Black Hills in South Dakota a few years. My
husband's father always gave his boys $2,000 when they started to
farm. But he wouldn't give my husband $2,000 because no sensible
person would try to farm in the Black Hills. So his father wrote that
there was a farm right across the road from theirs that he could get,
and if we would take it we'd get the $2,000. And we decided to
come back so we could get this farm and the $2,000, you know, and
so we could live in Wisconsin where the children would have good
schools and good churches, which they didn't have in the Black Hills.

We made the trip in a covered wagon. We could only get fifteen
dollars a head for our cattle and, oh, they were nice cattle. We
couldn't sell our horses for anything under the sun. So we made up
a four-horse team and had a younger horse that followed along with
us. We put our two-seated buggy behind our camp wagon. We had
a camp wagon with a bed in the back and another bed underneath it.
And sometimes my husband and the children slept outside and sometimes inside—it all depended on the mosquitoes. We came back to
Wisconsin in a covered wagon.

We were curiosities all the way across. Everyone was used to
seeing people going west, you know, but you never saw anybody
going east. And we would be going by a schoolhouse, and it would
be recess, and the kids would run along the side of the wagon and
sing, "Oh, look at the gypsies, look at the gypsies." Of course, we
were tanned like everything and we wore old clothes. That was
another trick. A lady who had done a good deal of traveling with a

family said, "Now, go to your rag bag and take out all those clothes you've got in there. They're good enough for a day or two in the camp wagon. Then throw 'em away." Well, of course, the environment was spoiled, but we didn't hear anything about the environment in those days, so you could throw away your old clothes. And that's the way we did. So we didn't have any old clothes when we got to Wisconsin; they had been disposed of. I feel kind of ashamed to tell it now, you know, but I was pretty glad to do it under the circumstances.

My husband died in 1910, and I raised the family alone from then on. I was father and mother both. But the children, as luck would have it, were pretty good. They didn't get into bad habits or do anything that was very terrible. And we got along very good.

But I had some rough spots. Yes, it was hard raising children alone. It ain't easy to talk about the rough spots, but it makes you appreciate the good spots. You had to keep them dressed. And they had to have clothes that were comparable to other children, you know. I could sew and I could make their clothes all right. But there was one year that I didn't have money enough to buy pencils and tablets to start my children to school. So I went to a neighbor's house and cleaned house, and I got two dollars for working all day. And I bought tablets and pencils and what they needed.

And that day my oldest son was going to go to the agricultural school in Madison. He was so delighted because he was ready to go. And he went up the silo, and when he got to the top step he missed it and went down, broke both of his ankles. For three months he had to be lifted from bed to chair to bathroom. Then the doctor bent one knee and put a wooden leg on that. And, oh, he was a wonderful doctor. He doctored my son, and he would bring boys out for him to see, and he would bring books for him to read. And after it was all over I felt pretty poor, but I went to ask the doctor how much it would cost—of course, I thought it would be in the hundreds. And I said, "Now, I haven't much money, but I've got plenty of hay that I can give you." And so he said, "Well, I don't know anything about it. I haven't looked at it. I'll look it up." And he went and looked in his book, and he said, "That's six dollars and a quarter." Well, of course I cried a little. Yeah, it was a problem to raise those children alone. But we got through some way.

For four years I taught school. Well, it was just a little country school. Little country desks. And a big belly stove right in the middle. And we went to the neighbors to get a pail of water, and we all drank out of the same dipper. And we didn't take any disease. And there was a wash dish on the bench there too. We had entertainment there, and the people all came. I had one boy that always rode a mule to school. Oh, that was fun! Then the kids could all ride the mule at recess.

In 1920, I started operating my boarding house. I sold the farm and I bought that house—prettiest house in River Falls. I had a relative that had remodeled it, and he came and said, "If you go to town, I've got just the house you want. There's six bedrooms in it and you can take roomers." Well, that looked good. And he made it easy for me to make the payments. So in 1920 I commenced to taking roomers. I took girls for a while, but they'd bring the boys in the house. And then I changed to just boys. And I've had some very fine boys, and I've had some of the meanest boys that ever lived. But the good ones were in a greater number than the poor ones.

And I ran that rooming house till a short while ago when I moved into this nursing home. And I think I'm very fortunate to have as comfortable a place as this in my declining years.

What are the bad things to you about being old?

Weak knees. Weak knees. That's the worst thing. I'm not real sure if my knees are going to hold me, you know. I fell down right over there because my feet commenced going this way, and I couldn't control them. I don't know why.

Oh, everything's changed. Everything has changed. You've got to—I don't know how to express it—you've got to accommodate to the change that goes on around you, some way or other. There's a good and a bad in all of it. And you can stay on the good side or you can drift across. But sometimes it's not so easy to decide which is the good and which is the bad.

❧ 104 ❧

Mr. BEN HYLKEMA
CUMBERLAND, WISCONSIN

Mrs. Susan Chakolis talks about her father:

He was born in Holland and came over here in his early twenties. He came with two brothers and a sister. First they went to Buffalo, New York, worked there, and then they came to Waukegan, Illinois. Then they heard of some reasonably priced wild land near Turtle Lake, Wisconsin, so he and his two brothers bought the land and built a little log house and started farming. There weren't any roads out there, so they had to build them. In 1898 a forest fire burned down the log house, so later on they built a big eight-room frame house and one of the biggest barns in that part of the country. They farmed and raised Holstein cattle. Farming meant everything to him. He got married to a woman who was also born in Holland, and had six children. My mother died twelve years ago. He lived in his own home until he was ninety-eight, and he recently rode as a special guest in our rutabaga parade.

My father was always a hard worker, and quite punctual, you know—everything went by the clock. He was very religious. He either went to church on Sunday or said prayers. He had European customs—like the man was the head of the family, you know. We went by what he said. And, as I recall, we women always took second place. I mean that was the European thing. He was very strict. We always had to go to bed at a certain time, very early. His discipline was never ever hitting. His discipline was silence. That hurt us.

And he was a very kind man, with animals especially. I recall how every animal meant so much to him. Every dog, every cat, every

113

horse were treated with great care. He was the veterinarian for the whole community. Anybody ever had a sick cow, they'd call him. And to this day, because of the way he was, we've all been such a lover of animals.

Mrs. ANNA WATSON
CRANSTON, RHODE ISLAND

Allen Watson describes his mother:

She was always a free-going mother. She never worried about much. You know, everything was always nice and happy. We never saw her lose her temper, even when we did a lot of funny tricks.

She was born in Germany. Her father owned and ran a snuff box factory over there. The snuff boxes were fancy things they had in those days. They were made of birch wood with metal edges and ivory on the top and fancy trimming on the corners. But they sold the factory, and the whole family came to this country to work in the mills. But she came over two or three years before the others in the family came. She was about fourteen when she came, and she came over with another family. In that neighborhood, in those days, if anybody was going to America and neighbor's children wanted to go, then they would take them over as their children.

When she first got here, she got a job as a waitress at the Slater Hotel in Pawtucket. And she still kind of talks about it to herself now, you know. She talks to Mr. Dorr; he's dead now, he was the superintendent of the Slater Mill, and she always waited on him. To wait on him, it was a big thing in her life. That's what she was saying a minute ago, asking Mr. Dorr what he wanted for dessert.

Mrs. Anna Watson on her wedding day.

Mrs. ANNIE CHRISTIAN
WALKER, MINNESOTA

My father was a sheriff and a musician. He played most any kind of instrument. My family were all more or less musicians. Violin or banjo, mouth organ, and we used to play the jews harp. I could play that, but I couldn't play nothing now. Not because I'm old; it's just because I'm dumb.

Yes, my father was sheriff of Carver County, Minnesota. And I can remember when the James brothers came to town—Jesse James. My father was sheriff, and he knew what was going on. He didn't know what Jesse James was going to do. So, my father came home and he said, "Now you crawl under the beds, you children, and don't you peek out and don't you dare come out. Because we don't know. There might be a lot of fighting and shooting. And we don't want you children hurt. Don't you come out from under there. You stay there." Well, they didn't do any harm there, but they went on to Northfield and robbed the bank. I like to talk of olden times. Just because I'm old, it's no sign I don't know.

Those were the days when the Indians were in Chaska. And there was a railroad trestle; it was built way up high for the train. And there was a train wreck. I don't know what caused the wreck, but the whole thing tipped over and barrels of apples fell out. And, oh, I don't know how many men were killed. The Indians, after a certain length of time, they asked my father if they could take some of those apples that were old and were all around. My father said, "You just go and get a basket or a barrel or anything and pick up all the apples you can get in. They're all yours. All you want." So I remember that in particular.

And when this railroad accident happened, of course, I wasn't old enough to understand it. Seven men in the crew were just laid out on boards. And it looked like to me one of the men had dirty gloves on. But it was his skin. Burned. I remember that very distinctly. I said to my father, "That man's got dirty gloves on." "No," he said, "he hasn't dirty gloves on, he's hurt badly." And my father said to my mother, "You better put that child in a buggy and take her away from here." I had seen too much. I wanted to see. I wasn't old enough to understand it. That man was scalded from the steam engine, and I thought he had dirty gloves on.

I was married sixty years.

Do you remember how you met your husband?

Oh, yes. He thought I was swell, for one thing . . . and I thought he was, too. And I said, "Well, what about it?" He said, "Oh nothing, only I think you're a pretty fancy girl." I said, "Thank you." And come to find out that he was living in the same block that I was. So that's how we became friends.

Mrs. Christian's daughter: Didn't you meet him in the skating rink?

Mrs. Christian: Oh, yes, but that was after that . . . So what's the difference where you meet him? Just so I *got* him.

Well, he was such a gentleman, you know, and nice, and I thought that was just fine. So then he tried to date me. And said, "Now wouldn't you like to go to the theater with me? *Mother's Love* is playing," if you remember that one. And it was a beautiful play. I was very much interested. And he was very nice. And I made up my mind I think that you're the man.

Will was my husband's name. He was a good, honest, Christian man, one of the most honest men I *ever* met in my life. And I think he was a perfect gentleman. I've had other friends, but I never cared for any of 'em. Anyway he was a very, very fine man. And he was that way all through life. He was always looking out for my welfare and that I was happy. That's why I had a long, happy life. Then we had children . . . and I brought 'em up the same way. Just be honest and careful who you associate with. And I said, "Remember, there's only one God. If you have any trouble, go to Him and He'll help you." Which has happened to me. Well, God's always with me . . .

and he is yet! Just wonderful! If I need anything or have anything sad I take it right to Him. I have *proof* in this building, this nursing home, about that. Someone that had a little deformity in some way, or sickness, I'd take it to God. . . . Anyway, life is worth living if you know how to handle it.

Do you think people are any different today from how they were in your young days?

Yes, I do. I think there's quite a difference. When I was a child, people seemed to be closer to one another than they are nowadays. But now you can't trust people, you can't trust everybody. Back then people were more friendly among themselves. And the family came first. You know, everybody had a good time. And if there was a dance, why, you took your family. Old folks, you know, took their kids to a dance. And your father or your mother would dance with you—the old Dutch dances. Oh, that was good times.

What do you do with your time?

I read a lot. And we're very busy visiting with people coming and going. They all stop right in this room. Everybody stops at my door—it doesn't make any difference whether it's man, woman, or child. I always have a little treat, a little candy, for the elderly people. They like that. And I like it too—there's no mistake about that.

And then this little lady that stays here, I read to her. You know, there's a girl that has to get me ready for bed. Why, she comes right after we have our supper. So she comes and fixes me up in bed with cushions and wheels me up. I can set up as late as I want to. Some of 'em fall asleep while I read to 'em. Well, most of the time I don't read to 'em, I just make up something, make up stories.

Could you tell me one of them?

. . . oh, I wouldn't dare tell some of 'em.

Well, I'm not so clever now. But I'm not going to give up! There's a lot of things that have to be done. There's something I have to do, but I don't know right now what it is. But I'm working, thinking and wondering. I want to figure it out to see whether it's right or whether it's wrong, which is the best way or how should it be. And

it takes time. I just lay and figure. I've always said I've got a lot locked up in here, but I just don't know how to figure it out. Sometimes I think until I can't think anymore. Isn't that silly? Well, maybe there'll be a way of finding out. I'm not living this life idle. I have to still work and find out. I lay awake all night long. Not because anything annoys me in the building, but I keep thinking. And I should let my brains rest; they've worked all my life. But there's things I want to know.

Your mind is very active, probably a lot more active than . . .

Well, why don't it open up and do something? Something's got to be done because I'm here for some reason or the Lord would have taken me. I know there's something that I haven't found out. But I'm going to *live* long enough to find out. I'm going to be 125.